Thirteen Promises

for Women In Sobriety

Thirteen Promises

For Uncle Bill and Auntie Lois
and Uncle Bob and Auntie Anne
and the women of Morning Glories
of Cambridge, Massachusetts

Table of Contents

Introduction — 5

1. If we are painstaking about this phase of our development we will be amazed before we are halfway through — 9
2. We are going to know a new freedom and a new happiness — 16
3. We will not regret the past nor wish to shut the door on it — 21
4. We will comprehend the word serenity and we will know peace — 26
5. No matter how far down the scale we have gone we will see how our experience can benefit others — 34
6. That feeling of uselessness and self-pity will disappear — 39
7. We will lose interest in selfish things — 45
8. Self-seeking will slip away — 49
9. Our whole attitude and outlook upon life will change — 53
10. Fear of people and of economic insecurity will leave us — 60
11. We will intuitively know how to handle things that used to baffle us — 67

12. We will suddenly realize that God is doing for us what we could not do for ourselves - 76
13. They are being fulfilled among us, sometimes quickly, sometimes slowly; they will always materialize if we work for them — 83

A Brief Guide to AA Jargon — 88
How To Pick Your First AA Meeting — 97
How To Start Your Own Promises Meeting — 107
Listen — 110
About — 115

Introduction

This book is based on one of the most famous passages from the book "Alcoholics Anonymous." Published in 1939, the Big Book is the basic text of the fellowship that bears its name. It outlines our program of recovery from alcoholism that has since been followed by millions and become the template for scores of other recovery programs.

This passage is called The Promises, and it appears on pages 83 and 84 in the fourth edition of AA's Big Book:

"If we are painstaking about this phase of our development, we will be amazed before we are halfway through. We are going to know a new freedom and a new happiness. We will not regret the past nor wish to shut the door on it. We will comprehend the word serenity and we will know peace. No matter how far down the scale we have gone, we will see how our experience can benefit others. That feeling of uselessness and self-pity will disappear. We will lose interest in selfish things and gain interest in our fellows. Self seeking will slip away. Our whole attitude and outlook on life will change. Fear of people and economic

Thirteen Promises

insecurity will leave us. We will intuitively know how to handle situations which used to baffle us. We will suddenly realize that God is doing for us what we could not do for ourselves. Are these extravagant promises? We think not. They are being fulfilled among us - sometimes quickly, sometimes slowly. They will always materialize if we work for them."

I was introduced to The Promises by the women of Morning Glories, a women's AA group that meets five days a week at 7AM. Each Friday, we discuss one of these thirteen promises. It was at that meeting that I first learned about what the program of AA promises to women who go to meetings, stay sober, and work the 12 steps. Much of what I have learned about living a sober life I learned from them -- but if you want to hear their stories, you will have to come to our meeting yourself. "Anonymity is the spiritual foundation of all our traditions," AA reminds us, and while I owe so much of what I know to others in this program, in this slender volume I stick to my own story and those of our founders as written in the Big Book.

I want you to know that I did not think the promises would come true for me. In fact, I did not think AA would work for me — not because I had anything against AA or people in AA — but because nothing else in my life had ever worked for me. Why would this work? Why would this help the constant misery, tension, and anxiety that I was never free of, that I drank to cope with? I had no faith that it would work, but I went ahead anyway, not knowing what else to do.

I want you to know that it did work.

I want you to know that you don't have to believe it will work for you to get it to work. You only have to put one foot in front of the other, stay sober, and work the steps to get it to work.

I want you to know that I believe in you, and I believe that if you are suffering today, either with active alcoholism or addiction or suffering even though you've gotten sober, that life can be good for you. I know this from my own experience and from the experience of countless others I have met in the rooms of Alcoholics Anonymous.

Lastly, before you read onward, I want to remind you that I am another alcoholic much like you. I'm just another bozo on the bus. If it's a tossup between listening to what your sponsor says and what you read here -- listen to your sponsor. As always, the final answer on our program lies between the covers of the Big Book. I hope we get to meet someday as we are trudging the Road of Happy Destiny.

Elle W.

1   *If we are painstaking about this phase of our development, we will be amazed before we are halfway through*

I was blubbering through yet another AA meeting — something I did often in early sobriety.

I hate crying in front of other people, but when I would raise my hand and share at meetings, I couldn't keep the tears back.

I want to say that this was not one or two tears rolling down my cheeks. This was ugly crying, the kind where you have to blow your nose in the middle. I doubt that anyone understood me after a sentence or two, not that my shares were long in the early days.

Afterwards, I'd sit in my seat mopping myself off with the box of Kleenex that was always offered me, feeling embarrassed but also a little lighter. Often I'd try to slink bashfully out of the room at the end of the meeting, but the men and women at this meeting would never let me.

On one particularly ugly-crying day, another member, a man named Kenny, came up to me after the meeting, put his hands on either side of my face, and said: "I can't wait to see the woman you're going to become."

I thought, "Why me? I'm just a screwup. I've messed up everything in my life — why would anyone feel that way about me?"

A few months later I arrived at the same meeting early and began putting out the chairs in the large hall. Kenny was the second person to show up, and joined me in setting up the room. I got up the courage to ask him: "Kenny, why did you say that to me?"

"Just because you're another alcoholic," he said.

Just because you're another alcoholic.

In recovery I realized I didn't have to be special, or perfect, or better or worse than anyone else in these rooms — I just had to show up and be honest. As time went on, I'd understand why Kenny had that faith: no one who stays long in the rooms of Alcoholics Anonymous can fail to notice the huge changes this program makes in the lives of people who commit to it. I came into AA with a sad, cynical belief that people didn't ever really change — but anyone who comes to meetings regularly will see people making dramatic changes for the better in their lives and families.

The Promises in the Big Book are, as any old-timer will point out, the Ninth Step promises — they're supposed to come true in our lives after we've completed steps One through Eight and begun making our amends to those we've harmed as part of Step Nine. Some might say that they only begin to materialize after we've completed all our amends.

If you're new in sobriety, I understand how that might feel like a very dim, distant, and uncertain prospect. I did not think The Promises even applied to me — I couldn't imagine ever getting that far. I believed I was different from other people — and not in a good way.

It has been my experience, and the experience of many I know, that some aspects of the Promises began to show up in their lives long before they approached the Ninth step. At 51 days sober, I had a new, good job; at 90 days sober I had a small but safe and bright place for my children. Even more important, I had had a taste of the peace and serenity this program offers to people who work hard at it.

I had what I later heard called "the gift of desperation." I did 90 meetings in 90 days. I didn't pick and choose between meetings: I just went. I got a sponsor on Day 3. I didn't sponsor-shop: I just got one. I called people on the phone. I went to meetings in strange cities when I traveled. I did whatever was necessary for me to get my butt in a chair at a meeting, every single day.

That wasn't easy. Like many women, I rarely said "no" when asked to do something, and I entered sobriety with a life that was completely unsustainable. I used alcohol not just to cope with feelings but to enable me to do more than I should have been doing. Alcohol was duct-tape holding my unmanageable life together. I could work long hours, work even more at home, and then use alcohol to wind down enough so I could sleep. Committing to going to a meeting every day, including the hour of the meeting itself, getting to and from the meeting, and making arrangements to be sure my kids were taken care of, was a major effort. I took to heart what one woman said in a meeting: "Anything in my life that is going to fall apart because I need to spend an hour a day making sure I don't drink myself to death is something I don't need in my life." Recovery is not something that we have to "fit into" our lives -- it's something that we must fit our lives around if we are to live lives of sane and happy usefulness.

"Whatever you put in front of your sobriety — job, relationship, money, family — will be the first thing you'll lose" is something I often heard in meetings. That didn't make it easier to put sobriety first. Looking back, I can see that putting sobriety first was an editorial process: one in which God was showing me what needed to be in my life, and what needed to be out.

In came hours of meetings, hours of work with my sponsor, reading, and hours spent listening to speaker tapes. I sometimes joked that I'd switched from NPR to DrunkPR). You might think I that because I believed in it: but I didn't. I often say in meetings that I didn't think the program would work for me, not because I had anything against AA or the people in it but because nothing else ever had. Why would this work? I'd read the Promises in the Big Book and I was glad they were there but I did not care if they ever happened to me. If they had put "Died Trying" on my tombstone, that would have been okay with me.

To get it to work I had to do things I didn't think would work. I had to do things I didn't understand, things I didn't believe in, things I didn't want to do, things I wasn't "ready for," things that made me uncomfortable, things I'd tried before that didn't work, things that pissed me off, things that made me cry, things that scared me.

None of these things were optional.

My ideas about how to run my own life did not work -- one look at the state it was in would tell anyone that. It didn't matter how I felt about the new ideas and habits that were being shown to me: it mattered that they worked.

I still go to a meeting every day, not because I have to but because I love them. I don't have a lot in the way of family. The women in the rooms are my family, the one I wished I had. Whenever I have a bad day, there's someplace for me to go. If it's three in the morning and I need to talk to someone, my phone is full of people who will take my call. On my Day 1 nobody would take my call and for damn good reason. Not today: today I can find support from my tribe of sober women, and give it, too.

I know if I want to stay sober I have to keep doing the things that got me sober. But my sober life is an amazing life, even when it's hard, and it is well worth the pains I take to keep it.

2 *We are going to know a new freedom and a new happiness*

When I talk to others about my story, I always try to remember what it was like before I got sober.

What I remember is this: while I didn't ever make plans to commit suicide, most days, when I got up, I'd feel like, "If a bus hit me, I'd be okay with that." I was tired. Tired of living the way I was. Tired of being me.

I was getting too tired to run from all the problems I'd piled up for myself while I was drinking -- problems I'd created by doing things I shouldn't have, or by not doing things I should have been doing. Good days -- ones in which everything went my way -- became farther and fewer between. Every day when I got up, I knew one of my problems was going to bite me in the ass. I just didn't know which one.

Getting sober made this worse, not better. Not only could I see my mountain of problems more clearly, but I wasn't anesthetizing my feelings about them anymore. I didn't know when or if I could solve them, or what would happen. I just had to wait, not drink, go to meetings, and do the next right action.

"Do the next right thing" was a phrase I often heard in the rooms. But there were many times where I didn't know what the next right thing was. In terror and bewilderment, I'd go to a meeting, raise my hand, and blurt out whatever was happening to me. I'm glad that I never had the feeling that I shouldn't raise my hand and participate in my own recovery in meetings, because when I did, I found something amazing: whatever problem I had, God had cleverly hid people in the rooms of Alcoholics Anonymous who had had the exact same experience and knew just what to do. It was uncanny -- whatever I did, and whatever was happening, I'd turn around and there someone would be, a stranger to me, who just happened to know the things I needed to know. My rule today is this: if I have a problem, I go to four AA meetings, raise my hand at every one, and talk honestly and specifically about my problem in detail. I've never even gotten to the third meeting before getting valuable information, and just as importantly, support and reassurance that if I stay sober everything will work out.

Going to meetings, not drinking, and asking for help gave me a freedom I'd never had -- freedom from years of problems I thought I would never untangle. Freedom from my own knee-jerk reactions -- yelling, lying, defensiveness, manipulation -- reactions I knew only got me in more trouble but that I'd previously felt helpless to change. Of course, it also gave me freedom from alcohol.

==I came into Alcoholics Anonymous not just not knowing how not to drink== -- I didn't know how to live. How was I to get along with others, be less of a jerk, be a good employee, parent, friend, and partner? I didn't know how to be happy, not for long. That's because I spent my entire life under the delusion that if everybody just did what I wanted, if everything just went my way -- then I'd be happy. Of course, that meant that whether or not I was happy was essentially as random as whether the weather would be sunny or rainy that day. I was giving up my ability to be happy and content to a world that wasn't going to do what I wanted when I wanted it. Despite that fact, I spent most of my days scrambling, scheming and manipulating to make things come out the way I wanted to.

Thirteen Promises

The most baffling thing was this: even when I did have everything I believed I wanted, I was rarely happy even then. When I arrived at this program, I had the advantage of knowing that my ideas about how to run my life didn't work. I supposed that my ideas about what made me happy had to be tossed on the trash heap, just like the ideas I had about how to run my life which had only served to run me into a ditch.

I would not have believed it if people told me that I would eventually find a way to have an inner happiness and contentment much of the time, even when things didn't go my way. But I'm far from the only person to have had this experience -- to go from the worst, most desperate period of my life to a life where my own feelings, attitudes and circumstances were so changed that I sometimes felt as if Old Me had died and I just inherited all her stuff. Uncle Bill, when writing down his story for us, says: "Everyone was resigned to the certainty that I would have to be shut up somewhere, or stumble along to a miserable end. How dark it is before the dawn! In reality, that was the beginning of my last debauch. I was soon to be catapulted into what I like to call the fourth dimension of existence. I was to know happiness, peace, usefulness, in a way of life that is

Thirteen Promises

incredibly more wonderful as time passes."

If you are new in sobriety, and you don't believe you will ever feel better, hang on until the miracle happens. The gifts of sobriety come: no one gets skipped. If you'd like the miracle to hurry up a little, make sure you are going to meetings, not drinking, and asking for help -- then make the move into your new life by joining a group, getting a sponsor, and working the steps. Remember: you don't have to wait to work the steps unless you want to wait to feel better.

3   *We will not regret the past nor wish to shut the door on it*

Just as my attitude about handling life's problems switched away from taking things outside myself -- mostly wine -- in a misguided attempt to make myself feel better when I didn't like how things were going, in sobriety my attitudes toward other people changed as well. I was the kind of alcoholic who drank a glass of wine in order to avoid fighting with their spouse, but then on the second (or third or fourth) glass forgot that that's why they were drinking, only to end up in an even uglier, alcohol-fuelled fight than ever. I was a mean drunk, and I was especially mean with my words.

In sobriety, I did not want the kind of arguments that went nowhere and felt awful in my life anymore, but I couldn't seem to start. Even sober, I was still going to every fight I was invited to. After one particularly poisonous argument with an ex, I realized something:

1. I argued with them even when I didn't want to and

was trying to avoid it.
2. Once I started arguing with them, I couldn't stop myself.
3. When I argued with them, I'd say and do things I was ashamed of.
4. After I argued with them, I'd have a literal, physical hangover afterward.

So how was it different from drinking?

It wasn't -- and that was why I had to put it down, just the way I put down the drink: one day at a time.

It wasn't easy. Sometimes it felt easier to stop drinking than it was to stop arguing with my ex! There were many, many days where I was Not Ripping Their Head Off Just For Today. Tomorrow -- tomorrow I can bowl with your head down Main Street, but not today-- not today!

What I found worked was that I simply stopped bringing my own emotions to our conflicts. I couldn't stop them from bringing theirs -- I couldn't control them -- but if I let them blurt out whatever feelings they had, without adding my own to the pile, the arguments generally just died out. I realized that conflicts are a dynamic: they require both people to contribute energy to them to keep going. Once I stopped giving them energy, they couldn't continue.

Many women in the rooms pointed out to me that there was no way to think my way into right action -- I had to act my way into right thinking. Just as they'd said, after a few months of right action, I no longer thought much about my conflicts with my ex; they were in the past. It was the beginning of a living amends process that continues to this day. It's amazing what not being a jerk, one day at a time, will do for even your most difficult relationships. While we may not want to be with people, and we may keep them at a distance to protect ourselves, we can always commit to not harming others even when we can't help them or be with them.

When we are new in sobriety, many of us desperately want to fix broken relationships, and will rush in with promises or try to pressure people who are angry and have been hurt by our behavior to talk to us and forgive us. When they reject us, not believing our promises or still stung by how we've hurt them, we are devastated or angry at them for not seeing how hard we are working and how we have changed. We don't always like to face the fact that we don't get to decide when or even if people will trust us again. All we can do is stay sober and do the next right thing; the rest is up to them and God.

It's worth reflecting on the fact that there might be reasons why people are no longer in our lives. Women who drink often develop unhealthy, twisted relationships, or become overly dependent on people when we should be standing on our own two feet and paying our own bills. Even though I knew that I was better off out of my relationship, I'd often listen to stories in meetings and think, "They did what? How come they got to keep their relationship and I didn't?" Then I'd talk to others in meetings and realize that maybe I had it easier: if I'd stayed in a sick relationship, would I be sober and sane today? Probably not.

We must commit to staying sober whether people come back into our lives or not. The Big Book reminds us that we should never let anyone say that they cannot recover unless their family comes back: "This just isn't so…remind the prospect that his recovery is not dependent upon people. It is dependent upon his relationship with God. We have seen men get well when families have not returned at all. We have seen others slip when the family came back to

We can obsess over family members, spouses, or friends who won't come back, instead of accepting it and living a sober life and allowing them to come back or not on their own terms. But we must remember that we cannot make amends to anyone if we are not respecting their wishes for themselves, even if their wish is to not see us, talk to us, or be around us.

What if we weren't in a relationship when we got sober? We will hear in the rooms that we should wait a year before getting into a new one. We could rebel against this idea — but how we react to these situations is often the biggest test of whether we're truly willing to put our program first. Are we truly willing to put our program first, live a sober life, and do the next right thing regardless of what anyone does or says? Are we willing to stay sober with or without a relationship?

4 We will comprehend the word serenity and we will know peace

When I got sober, my problems had problems. And as alcoholics, well...we pile up problems: family problems, job problems, problems with the courts, financial problems, problems with the former husband or current girlfriend, with our cars, with our living situation — you name the problem, an alcoholic has had it.

Writing in the Twelve & Twelve, Uncle Bill calls us "a problem people." But he goes on to say that "We have been talking about problems because we are problem people who have found a way up and out, and who wish to share our knowledge of that way with all who can use it. For it is only by accepting and solving our problems that we can begin to get right with ourselves and with the world about us."

The hard part is this: when we come into sobriety we often have problems that look like this: we don't know when they'll be solved, how they'll be solved, or if they'll be solved. Yet we have to stay sober in the not-knowing, which is one of the hardest things in the world.

Maybe the marriage is broken for good (mine was). Maybe the court case won't go our way. Maybe we won't get the job in time to pay the rent, or the apartment in time to avoid not knowing where we're going to live. Maybe we won't be able to stay in school, or get out of that relationship fast enough because we don't have a place lined up to stay yet. Maybe those frightening letters from the IRS really mean what they say.

Perhaps you are like me, or like one of so many others who feel like they are trying to get sober in a shitstorm.

You are not alone.

I remember being upset about something in early sobriety — I can't recall exactly what it was, but I was going through a messy, contentious divorce at the time — and talking to my sponsor about it. She said, "See? God got you sober just in time." I thought, "Really?! I think I picked a terrible time to stop drinking and killing myself!" Of course, she was correct: had I been drinking, everything would have been so much worse; there's no telling how things might have turned out.

There were many times in those early days that I was so upset that my scalp would tingle and sweat. I'd look at the orange numbers of the clock above the stove and think: "In twenty minutes I won't feel this way." There were some days in early sobriety — many days — where "one day at a time" was too damn long. I didn't want to drink: I just didn't know how to get through that day.

On nights when I could not sleep, I'd take a miniature copy of the Big Book I'd been given at a meeting, and I'd read the Promises. At that point, I did not care if they ever came true for me. I did not believe that they would, and in any case, I knew from listening in meetings that the Promises were the Ninth Step Promises, and there was a yawning gulf between me and that step. It was going to take a very long time for me to make amends to all the people I'd hurt.

Each day brought fresh hurts. I couldn't concentrate; I couldn't tell you how I was going to feel fifteen minutes from now; I had terrible, vivid dreams. I went to a meeting each day, sometimes more than once a day, desperately trying to hang on even though I didn't really believe that anything would get better.

I didn't think this program would work for me. That's not because I had anything against AA, against the steps, or against people I met in the rooms. I didn't think it would work for me because nothing else had ever worked for me. I was a tense, anxious, depressed kid who had grown into a tense, anxious, depressed adult. I'd tried everything to fix what was happening with me between my ears: meditation, medication, therapy, sex, drugs, and rock and roll (though as a shy nerd, I mostly skipped that last one). Some helped a little. But nothing helped very much. No matter what I did, I was still stuck with me: with my misery, my resentments, my fears. In many ways, alcohol was the thing that helped the most to quiet the constant racket of fears and angers in my head; that's one big reason why I drank. Not drinking didn't make it better: it made it worse, in part because I wasn't anesthetizing myself and in part because I could see the mountain of wreckage I'd made clearly because I wasn't drinking.

I had never felt "okay." I don't remember feeling okay as a kid. In many ways I'm surprised I waited as long as I did to drink.

I didn't expect the program to help me with this. When I came in, I was a basket case. I knew I had to take the wine out of the basket, because that was causing problems. Oh, and the basket was on fire, and if you could help with that, that would be great. But when I'd read the steps on the wall, like the Promises, I didn't think they applied to me or would help me, so when I read Step 2 — "Came to believe that a power greater than ourselves would restore us to sanity," I didn't think that would happen to me, that anything could or would help me.

But something happened to me in early sobriety.

One morning when I was about two months sober I woke up in the guest room of the house I lived in with my soon-to-be ex-husband. It was a bright and sunny morning in early July.

I opened my eyes and looked out the windows at the beautiful morning, and it was quiet in my head.

It was quiet in there.

Thirteen Promises

This was such an unfamiliar and frightening experience for me that my first response to it was, "Did I die?" I thought maybe this is like one of those movies where I'll get up from the bed and my body will stay there while my soul floats around the room.

I heard voices and movement in the house, and that convinced me I wasn't dead. But I had such an overwhelming feeling that something had happened inside my head that my next thought was: "Did I have a stroke?"

I wiggled both my feet in bed. Nope, I hadn't had a stroke.

And then I lay there. I didn't want to move, because I thought that feeling would go away. It was like a butterfly had landed on my nose.

I had just had my first experience of the peace and serenity that this program promises.

Who did that to me? Who calms the waters? Who dwells within the peace that passes understanding? Who quieted the ceaseless racket of fears and hurts inside my head?

Sometimes I believe that I got it when I did because Someone or Something knew that if I didn't get something that I wasn't going to be able to hang on.

I can't say that I feel that way all the time now — but I know that it's down there all the time now. I pile crap on top of it — and I have to use both common sense, restraint, saying sorry, and other things this program has taught me to scrape it off — but I know that it is always available to me if I work for it. I could have dug to China in therapy, done all the yoga in the world, chugged Ayahuasca with a shaman in the rainforest, or won the lottery and not have had this feeling before that moment. It simply wasn't available to me. And it only became available once I came into this program. I don't understand how it works, or why, but I do know it only happened when I got and stayed sober and committed to staying that way even if I never felt better.

Like everyone else, I have the same jolts and disappointments that life offers. But I have more peace and serenity on a daily basis than I ever remember having, even as a child. It is a regular feature of my life today, and I am very grateful for it.

Thirteen Promises

5 *No matter how far down the scale we have gone, we will see how our experience can benefit others*

Note that the promise does not say: "If we have gone all the way down to the bottom of the scale, we will see how our experience can benefit others." We can be helpful to others no matter where we decided to step off alcoholism's elevator to life's sub-basement.

Confusion about what "hitting bottom" really means keeps a lot of women out of recovery.

Sometimes a woman who is scared about her drinking but who hasn't experienced a lot of external consequences will go to a meeting, listen to someone's story, and walk right out of AA thinking, "I haven't gotten a DUI. I haven't lost my kids, my job, or my marriage. I haven't ended up in jail. I'm just not like these people."

What she may fail to grasp is this: alcoholism is a progressive illness. What that means is that over any significant period of time, it gets worse. Even if a woman is able to stop or moderate for awhile, if she is truly an alcoholic, her drinking, and the consequences for that drinking, will get worse over the months and years. Short improvements don't change the fact that the trend line is invariably downward, sometimes quickly, sometimes slowly. Those women in the meeting who experienced lots of consequences as a result of her drinking aren't different from her: they are her Coming Attractions. Many of us don't need to go to a meeting to get a look at those coming attractions: we have a mom, or a dad, or others in our family who give us a peek into where active alcoholism will bring us.

Too many of us define alcoholism by those very consequences. But saying someone only has a problem if they've lost a job, marriage, or their driver's license, or even their kids, is simply a recipe for more women to experience those very consequences.

And many, many women find out the hard way that they were much closer than they realized to those big consequences all along.

There are also women who have experienced jail, losing custody of their kids, losing jobs and relationships, homelessness or institutionalization. In particular, women who also suffer from mental illness, or come from families or relationships where they were abused may feel they are "too broken" for getting sober to matter.

Any woman who is even contemplating getting sober has had years of practice justifying and defending her drinking. "He's worse than I am -- he's the one with the real problem." "I have anxiety and depression. That's why I drink." "I'm not really that bad." "Real alcoholics are physically addicted. I'm sure I'm not." "I really don't drink that much. A real alcoholic drinks much more than I do." Add to these a raft of ideas telling ourselves that alcoholism isn't our real problem, that AA is a cult, too religious, not for smart people, not scientific enough. That there must be some way of getting sober that doesn't require sacrifices, or that the real problem is the job, the relationship, the family, and if that was all straightened out we wouldn't drink the way we do.

Like every alcoholic, I got sober only to find that my mind was jam packed with ideas -- ideas that if I believed them, it was okay to drink. Either I wasn't so bad, or I was too far gone to bother stopping. Each of these thoughts had a job description, and their job description read, "Get her to drink." And I had to fire each and every one of them as they showed themselves to me. Once we are convinced that our drinking is a problem, there are no real "reasons" to drink -- only excuses.

I have come to believe -- and in time, you may too -- that I am no different, and absolutely no better -- than any woman whose bottom was worse than mine. A true "bottom" is a spiritual matter, waving a white flag deep down in our soul, saying, "I can't do this anymore."

Whatever kind of bottom we have -- high bottom, low bottom -- really doesn't matter. For far too many women, the only bottom they find is the dark, cold bottom of the grave. Alcoholism kills three women an hour in the United States. There are no empty seats in the rooms of Alcoholics Anonymous: they are filled with the souls of people who couldn't get this thing, or having gotten it, couldn't keep it.

Seen from this perspective, there are really only two types

of bottom: the kind above the grass, and the kind below it.
If you are reading these words, you got the good kind.
Hang on to it.

6 *That feeling of uselessness and self-pity will disappear*

"We were having trouble with personal relationships, we couldn't control our emotional natures, we were a prey to misery and depression, we couldn't make a living, we had a feeling of uselessness, we were full of fear, we were unhappy, we couldn't seem to be of real help to other people..." This passage from the Big Book is known as The Bedevilments, and it's a pretty good description of my life at the end of my drinking. I couldn't seem to get anything right. I began each day with a sense of impending doom. I'd piled up a lot of problems for myself with my drinking, and I knew one of them was going to bite me in the ass — I just didn't know which one.

As time went on, my drinking got worse, and the sense of doom was joined by a sense of fatigue. I was getting too worn out to keep running from my troubles. I was tired, and I could hear the hoofbeats of what our book calls The Four Horsemen of alcoholic doom swiftly approaching behind me — terror, frustration, bewilderment, despair.

And yes, I felt useless. And I felt bad for myself. These, I later learned, were common afflictions among alcoholics, the logical outcome of an alcoholic way of life that saps our strength, our courage, and our willingness to face the truth about ourselves.

Many us, before we get sober, felt useless because we were useless: if you brought us a problem, you had two problems. We couldn't help — we'd probably make things worse, or just yell at you for daring to have a problem. Or perhaps we are the sort of alcoholic who used our work at home or on the job as a way to say we "deserved" to drink. Maybe we even blamed others for being "useless" at home or at the workplace and used those resentments to fuel more drinking. Maybe we bolstered ourselves with talk of how hard we worked and how many responsibilities we had, but deep down, we knew we weren't really taking care of things the way we knew we should. Fear not: you are far from the only woman to drink "at" the boss, the partner, the family. But be sure to know this: recovery begins where blame ends. We cannot get well by blaming others for our circumstances.

Self-pity can't be eliminated only once, though. Like a weed, it will return, and we'll have to deal with it when it crops up. One day I found myself really down about something. I called my sponsor and asked, "I know our program tells us we're supposed to eliminate self-pity, but what are we supposed to do if we feel bad for ourselves?"

She responded, "You get a big hug." So perhaps this is useful — after all, we need a way to move on from self-pity and into a realistic assessment of ourselves and our part in bringing about whatever it is that's making us feel bad for ourselves.

But compassion must be combined with action if we are to get over our self-pity. That same sponsor, when reviewing my inventory of resentments with me, called the Fourth Step "the step where we take our power back." As sober women, we are not helpless, useless victims of life and circumstance; we are not women to be pitied. We have a way out of that mindset and the life it creates through the process of fourth step inventory. Wherever we see a way in which we participated in a situation that's now bringing us down, that's an avenue for us to bring about change in our lives and ourselves.

It's not always fun or comfortable to see my part in my resentments. I'm a real grudge-hugger, and I'd love for everything to be all their fault. But the Big Book brings us up short when we try to pass off our resentments as others victimizing us. In fact, they caution us that by indulging in self-pity, we may be manufacturing future hurts: "Driven by a hundred forms of fear, self-delusion, self-seeking, and self-pity, we step on the toes of our fellows and they retaliate. Sometimes they hurt us, seemingly without provocation, but we invariably find that at some time in the past we have made decisions based on self that placed us in a position to be hurt."

Simply knowing that we need and want to eliminate self-pity and the feeling of uselessness from our lives as sober women doesn't mean we know exactly how to go about it, however. The good news is that our book has specific and concrete directions for doing just that, from getting off to a good start in the morning, staying on track throughout the day, and even emergency procedures for really bad days: "As we go through the day we pause, when agitated or doubtful, and ask for the right thought or action. We constantly remind ourselves that we are no longer running the show, humbly saying to ourselves many times a day, "Thy will be done." We are then in much less danger of excitement, fear, anger, worry, self-pity, or foolish decisions."

But how can we possibly avoid self-pity when things in our lives truly are tough? Bill shows us that being useful to another alcoholic in the unique way that only an alcoholic can is in itself a prescription to help us out of the swamp of self-pity: "My wife and I had abandoned ourselves with enthusiasm to the idea of helping other alcoholics to a solution of their problems. It was fortunate, for my old business associates remained skeptical for a year and a a half, during which I found little work. I was not too well at the time, and was plagued by waves of self-pity and resentment. This sometimes nearly drove me back to drink, but I soon found that when all other measures failed, work with another alcoholic would save the day."

Remember that *our primary purpose is to stay sober and help another alcoholic.* It is not to pay bills, or get the right job, relationship, house, number on the scale, inner peace, or arrive at some place in our lives where we have no problems. Our purpose is both much larger and much more simple than that. In difficult times, we must cling to that purpose all the more; when times get tough, we must keep our program tight — attending meetings, calling our sponsors, being of service to other alcoholics. Difficulties at work or at home, or just being busy with the life you've managed to gain in sobriety are the worst possible excuses for going to fewer meetings or letting your network of sober women slide. Those are the very times when you will need your program the most. Don't kid yourself that going to fewer meetings, or slacking off on the steps is safe. We should only pause in our program or the steps if we want our lives to stall, too: they are inextricably linked. Go to a meeting each day for a week and you're virtually guaranteed to hear the story of someone who relapsed because they started to do the work only when it was convenient for them. A relapse is surely a fast trip back to that feeling of uselessness and self-pity. You deserve better than a chutes-and-ladders sobriety. Keep at your program, keep climbing, and take other women with you on the path.

7 *We will lose interest in selfish things and gain interest in our fellows*

When I got into recovery, I hated myself.

Let me amplify that a bit: I hate, hate, HATED myself.

I remember walking around with a thirty day chip, and then a sixty day chip, walking down the sidewalk, hating myself. I'd hold the chip tightly in my hand and repeat to myself in my head, "I can't change the past. I can only live right today."

I'd done the kind of damage that couldn't be undone, said things that couldn't be un-said. I was a mean, angry drunk.

I wasn't sure what I could do to heal that wound, but I can say today that I don't hate myself; it is healed, and I'll tell you how it happened.

One day in early sobriety, I was sitting around at work hating myself. And I listened to a radio program hosted by a friend of mine. He was interviewing someone about veterans returning from Iraq, and they were talking about a concept I'd never heard of before. It was called "moral injury."

Moral injury is the injury you get when you do something that violates your own sense of right and wrong. The symptoms of that injury are shame, disconnection, and self-hatred.

Like a lot of people, I did myself a fair amount of moral injury before I got sober. And I suffered from the symptoms of feeling ashamed, disconnected, worse than and different from other people, and punishing self-hatred.

I wasn't able to get my self-esteem back by giving myself a big hug, or reciting affirmations in the mirror -- it didn't work. I heard someone say, "if you want self-esteem, do esteemable acts," and I thought, why don't I give that a try? At first, I didn't actually feel like I had a lot to give, but since I was sober I did remember how to bake.

When I was still drinking, I couldn't hold it together long enough to bake cookies: I'd put one batch in the oven, burn it, curse as I scraped the burnt cookies off the baking sheet and into the trash, put in another batch…and burn that one too! With that batch I'd curse even more because I'd usually set off the smoke alarm. I had a uniquely alcoholic solution to the problem with the smoke detectors: I took out the batteries.

However, in sobriety I regained a number of key skills, among them being the ability to remember to set the kitchen timer.

I was living in a new place, having split with my former partner, and that was a huge adjustment for my two school-age children. I cooked and baked to put routine in their lives; I baked the same cookie recipe every week for a year so that their house would smell amazing each time they returned from their father's house. But I also baked things for meetings.

At the time, I went to a few meetings a week that met in a hospital where there was a detox ward. The patients coming down from the ward to the meeting looked like they hadn't seen a cupcake in A LONG TIME. I used to like to sit somewhere I could see the food table and watch people realize, "HEY CUPCAKES!" and I would feel just a tiny little feeling of being happy about something I did, which isn't something I'd felt for a long, long time.

Then one day sitting there, I thought: "What if I tried to be as nice to everybody as I am to a perfect stranger in a meeting?" That seemed pretty radical, because "everybody" included my soon to be ex-husband, who at that point I hated and feared. But whatever, I brought him some cupcakes. He looked like I might be trying to poison him, which introduced me to the fun of being nice to people who don't expect you to be nice to them: it messes with their minds a little, and that's hilarious.

I stayed sober; when I promised something to my kids I kept my promise; I showed up to work and tried to give good value for the money they were paying me. I tried to be helpful to people when I could. And that just became a habit.

And I don't know exactly when, but one day I realized I didn't hate myself anymore.

8 Self seeking will slip away

"God, I offer myself to Thee To build with me & to do with me as Thou wilt. Relieve me of the bondage of self, that I may better do Thy will. Take away my difficulties, that victory over them may bear witness to those I would help of Thy Power, Thy love & Thy way of life."

"The bondage of self." That's a remarkable phrase, isn't it? It occurs nowhere else in the Big Book, nor does it appear in Twelve Steps & Twelve Traditions, but it does appear in this passage, which is known as the Third Step Prayer.

The bondage of self is a terrible predicament: in it we are consumed by our wants and our problems. Losing the job, getting the apartment, that court date, the family trouble, those debts, that ominous sound the car is making, whether we'll ever get our license back, that letter from the IRS, the text from the ex, will we get into that program, will they find out, will they stop using, why don't they see it my way?

These are all self-centered fears: fears that we'll lose what we have, and that won't get what we want.

When I give an honest answer to the question, "Am I a

slave to self-centered fear today?" the answer is often not what I would like.

The good news is that in sobriety I have experienced freedom from these fears. That's not because I have any more control over the world than I did the day I got sober. It's because I have control over whether I allow my mind and my actions to be all about me.

Self-seeking is different from selfishness: selfishness is about wanting more than my fair share; self seeking is being all about me, 24 hours a day. If there's a more effective, or more awful prison than being trapped in my own head with my resentments, fears, self-pity, and self-hatred, I don't ever want to experience it.

But how do we escape from the bondage of self?

Fortunately, our alcoholic ancestors left some directions. "On awakening let us think about the twenty-four hours ahead. We consider our plans for the day. Before we begin, we ask God to direct our thinking, especially asking that it be divorced from self-pity, dishonest, or self-seeking motives."

If you're like me, that's a good start, but it doesn't get you through the whole day. Hell, it rarely gets me through a morning before I'm right back to I, Myself, and Me and My Problems.

I need more than that, which is why I go back to basics and stay there — back to the things I heard from people early on in sobriety. "Just stay sober and everything will be all right, even if you don't see it now." "Don't drink, go to meetings, and ask for help," they said. "Wrap your day around a meeting." "Help another alcoholic."

The royal road out from the bondage of self is service to others. If you have not tried this for yourself, do so! At your lowest moment, when you feel you have nothing to give anyone, when you feel dumb, when you feel like a loser, when you feel like you'll never get it right, working with others will show you that you always have something to offer another alcoholic. None other than Bill W. did this: "Many times I have gone to my old hospital in despair. On talking a man there, I would be amazingly lifted up and set on my feet. It is a design for living that works in rough going."

I have come to feel that my recovery is not exclusively or even primarily about me; I am a small part of something much larger, but that does not mean that I am not essential.

Everything we do for one another in the service of our recovery together counts. We are getting one another free: free from the prison of alcoholism, and into a bigger, freer life that's about more than just us.

We are not alone anymore, which is a wonderful gift that comes to us when we begin to put ourselves in service to the God that doesn't want alcoholics like us to live and die alone in the degrading misery of active addiction. There's a bonus gift, too: we find that we don't have to be special, unique, or better or worse than anyone else to belong and be useful. You can discover the joy of being Just Another Bozo on the Bus. There is no overachieving in AA, no grades or trophies to be given out. You don't have to have the worst bottom or the best drunkalogue. You don't have to know the Big Book by heart — you just have to read it. You don't have to be a star at working the steps, you just have to do them. You just have to show up and be honest — and you'll find that just those simple things will help you do something that really is special and unique: you can actually save another woman's life with them.

9   *Our whole attitude and outlook upon life will change*

I was very lucky when I got sober: the obsession for alcohol was removed from me fairly quickly. I did not go to a detox, although I probably should have -- I had no idea alcohol was dangerous. As a result, I detoxed in the rooms of Alcoholics Anonymous, where I drank a lot of weapons-grade AA coffee, ate a lot of cheap cookies, and cried.

The way I drank, I believe I did things to my brain that took time to heal. It was difficult for me to decipher the meeting book -- all those little addresses and acronyms bewildered me. I could read, but when I finished a page, I couldn't remember what I'd just read. I was on the Olympic Nap Team for the first six months. Dealing with life unfiltered is exhausting in the beginning. I had strange, vivid, disturbing dreams. I had terrible mood swings: I couldn't tell you how I'd feel fifteen minutes from now. While those mood swings diminished in the first few months, in the first year I experienced sharp, short depressions that lasted only a few days but were terrifyingly intense, as if drinking had worn out the shock absorber on my brain, or, perhaps, my soul.

But I wasn't drinking, and I wasn't hungover, and that meant I could tackle my problems, fill out a form, clean my house, be a gentle, present, loving parent for my kids, go to work on time, cook a meal, keep myself in clean clothes, and generally stay out of trouble. Gentle entertainments and plenty of rest helped me a lot in the beginning and still do today when I need them. I planted a garden; I took up an interest in making the kind of blankets I remember my grandmother and her sisters making.

And in general, I had few urges to drink. That didn't mean I didn't see alcohol in my world: boy, did I ever. I seemed more aware of it than ever before, and it seemed to be absolutely everywhere: in grocery stores, on billboards, on advertisements plastered on buses, in lighted signs in restaurant windows. I even noticed alcohol in places that began to seem inappropriate or even creepy -- on t-shirts proclaiming that "Wine is Mommy Juice," and once on a sparkly greeting card that read: "It's not drinking alone if you're with your kids." When out at a restaurant, the stacked bottles and rows of taps bothered me, and I'd often try to put my back to them so I wouldn't see them, only to find that there was a mirror in front of me, and there they were, all those bottles again.

But one day, even though nothing had changed, everything changed for me: alcohol became invisible to me. It didn't bother me to go out to a restaurant where alcohol was being served. I knew the signs and advertisements were still there, but they just didn't register with me anymore. I still didn't keep alcohol in my house, but not because I was afraid I'd drink it. In addition to the run of the mill lying, cheating and stealing most alcoholics do, I'd done emotional harm to people who cared about me -- I'd robbed them of their peace of mind. By this time, my house was a clean, safe place with cold cuts and an XBox where friends, neighbors, and friends of my kids hung out. I knew if a friend came to my house and opened the refrigerator to find wine or beer, they'd get a nasty jolt even if I wasn't drinking. I feel I've lost my right to rob people who love me of their peace of mind today.

In that first year, my big job was finding ways to discover and honor my sober limits. Most of us have heard "HALT" in the rooms, used as an acronym for Hungry, Angry, Lonely, Tired. So many situations that were driving us to drink early on seemed mysteriously, almost magically solved or at the very least rendered manageable by the application of a healthy snack, a call with a sponsor, an AA meeting, or a nap. One way my attitude changed was how I approached difficult situations in sobriety: when waves of emotion would hit me that were too big for me to handle, I heard from other women in the program that I could do anything I wanted -- anything at all -- if it would make me feel better and it wasn't destructive or self-destructive. This of course left out screaming fights with exes or family members, and anything self-destructive or self harming, which absolutely meant no drinking or drugs.

Initially, I had no idea where my sober limits were, or where they should be: I only discovered them by barking my shins on them in the dark. I knew when I was outside my sober limits because I'd feel crazy, thirsty, or both. I also saw many, many women in the rooms who continued to kid themselves about where their sober limits were. "Sure, I can stay in that relationship even though they still use." "But I have to go to that conference or work party!" "I can stay in this crazy making job and not drink. I just won't drink, that's all." "I know my sponsor says to go to 90 meetings in 90 days but I just don't have time for that. I can be this busy and not drink." "Everybody says not to get in a relationship in the first year, but they're sober too, so it will actually help me stay sober."

We can kid ourselves all we want about our sober limits: we just can't do it and stay sober and sane. We're either willing to respect those limits or we aren't.

If I'm honest, I don't always like where my sober limits are. I look at someone else and say, "Normal people can do it, why can't I?" The truth is, it's none of my business where my sober limits are: it's God's business. If they change, when they change, or whether they change at all is neither up to me nor any of my business. My business is to discover and accept them, and live a good life inside them.

Sober limits, however, cannot be a reason to avoid legitimate adult responsibilities. Court dates, dealing with our taxes, exes, and adult life is not optional. All of us will have to walk through fear, heartbreak, and anger in sobriety, and not drink. But how? Another sober woman gifted me the idea of "bookending" — putting a meeting or a call with another sober woman before and after a difficult experience. In the past, it might have been our way to go it

Thirteen Promises

alone — but we have to change our ways and realize that isolation is dangerous in sobriety.

Changes in attitude and outlook may happen suddenly or gradually -- but maintaining our new way of looking at ourselves, others, and the world is a lifetime practice that requires vigilance. As an example, one of my great sources of happiness in sobriety has been being able to do things with my loved ones that give all of us happy memories to look back on. I was able to save to take a trip with my sons to a faraway city they had never visited. We enjoyed the sights, visited museums, ate enormous ice cream sundaes, and just enjoyed one another's company. We laughed so much! But in this faraway city, I noticed something disturbing: the lighted signs advertising alcohol, the billboards, the signs on buses, the sandwich boards advertising happy hour that had been invisible to me for so long were suddenly visible again. It was creepy: I almost felt as if the alcohol was watching me, waiting for me to let my guard down for a minute so it could get me.

But because of my program, I knew that I should respond to thoughts of drinking just like I should respond to the warning lights on my car's dashboard -- I shouldn't ignore them, I should do something about them! I called my sponsor and went to a meeting in that faraway city. Not only did I meet new friends -- when I left I noticed that the lights advertising booze were out again.

10 Fear of people and of economic insecurity will leave us

The Ninth Step is the culmination of a process that will allow us to walk down any street or supermarket aisle in the world without cringing, no matter who we may meet. The work isn't easy, though. Many alcoholics never get to Step Nine because they have a fear of Steps Four and Five — where we write down our inventory and share it with another human being.

But what do our lives look like when we don't face up to our own behavior and commit to changing it? I've seen what my life is like without Steps Four and Five. When I don't take my inventory, it ends up getting taken by my ex-husband's divorce lawyer. What that says to me is what a gift it is to be able to take our own inventory and share it with someone we trust. If we do not take our own inventory, someone else will — and it's likely that the people doing it will be the very people we have hurt. Thank god we get to take our own inventory! Thank God we get to

Thirteen Promises

tell it to a sponsor! We've all seen the alternatives, and they aren't nearly as gentle.

Most of us come into sobriety with a lot of fear and anger towards others. In the Big Book, our uncle Bill writes: "Driven by a hundred forms of fear, self-delusion, self-seeking, and self-pity, we step on the toes of our fellows and they retaliate. Sometimes they hurt us, seemingly without provocation, but we invariably find that at some time in the past we have made decisions based on self which later placed us in a position to be hurt."

I had good reason to be afraid of people when I was still drinking: my drinking put me in the orbit of people it wasn't safe to be around. I'd also pissed a lot of people off through my thoughtless, self-centered, and sometimes cruel behavior. One of my biggest fears in early sobriety was that I'd lose custody of my children. Of course, I was angry at and fearful of their father, who I thought would do this. But I'd created the conditions for that fear through my treatment of him and my reckless behavior.

It took years of living amends — staying sober, living right each day, and refraining from retaliating, harming, or yelling at him before our relationship became even remotely friendly. Amends in the form of an apology wouldn't have meant much early on, as he had heard enough of my apologies and promises to change. As an early mentor of mine in the program said: "An apology isn't an amends — an amends mends things." The damage we do to others and our relationships often can't be mended with a simple apology: it can take years of patient work and self-restraint to heal them and many such relationships will never be the same.

But today, the people I feared the most when I first got sober I no longer fear. Committing to being sober, refraining from harming or lashing out at others, and committing fully to the 12 steps including 9th step amends has left me nothing to fear.

But what about economic uncertainty? As I write these words, I am experiencing that insecurity — as I imagine some of you reading these words are, too. Nine months after getting what seemed to me to be a dream job, I learn that the organization I am working for is running out of money for the project I was hired for.

Thirteen Promises

What will happen? Will I be out of work? Will I be able to keep my job here or get a job somewhere else? What if I am out of work a long time?

As so many women in this program have told me, even though we are sober now, life keeps happening, good and bad. Even our founders experienced adversity after getting sober. After having cratered his career with his drinking, once Bill W. was sober he got a shot at some work:

"Years ago, in 1935, on of our number made a journey to a certain western city. From a business standpoint, his trip came off badly. Had he been successful in his enterprise, he would have been set on his feet financially, which, at the time, seemed vitally important. But his venture wound up in a law suit and bogged down completely. The proceeding was shot through with much hard feeling and controversy.

I think many of us have felt his feelings after something we'd hoped for doesn't go our way: "Bitterly discouraged, he found himself in a strange place, discredited and almost broke."

And when this happens, he is standing in a hallway: a hallway between a bar and a telephone where he can talk to

Thirteen Promises

another alcoholic.

I think that perhaps we are all always in the hallway between the bar and the phone; it's just most obvious to us when we are in those tough situations that life hands us.

Even today, I have to decide: which direction am I going to go? Towards connecting with my fellow alcoholics? Or the other direction? And I only fool myself if I think there is a third direction. There isn't. I am always either going toward or away from a drink, and that decision is never more critical than when times are tough.

Because of this program I can be calmer about changes that may come, because I knew that whatever trouble I face, I can go to a meeting of my fellow alcoholics and ask for support, not just for my drinking but for the problems of living a good sober life. I know that I am not alone in the world, and this makes all the difference in my life, my behavior, and my spirit. My first sponsor used to say that our program had a special promise for the women of Alcoholics Anonymous: that we were going to be women of honor and dignity. If that's true, our honor and dignity must come from something other than the job, the relationship, the home, the car, all the things of the world that can go away in an instant. Our literature tells us this, saying that once we have committed to the work of sobriety that "We had a new Employer. Being all powerful, He provided what we needed, if we kept close to him and performed his work well." That work — staying sober and helping another alcoholic — is not something that we can get laid off from.

When I raise my hand in a meeting and talk honestly about what's happening with me, what my fears are, where I am confused, I discover again the truth that God has cleverly hidden everything I will ever need to know about handling life on life's terms inside the minds of people in meetings of Alcoholics Anonymous. One of the main things I need to know is that people have been through similar situations, yet here they stand in front of me, where I can see for myself that they are still sober, and that they went through that experience and they are okay today. Seeing that they survived it gives me hope that I can survive it too.

If we have money troubles or job troubles, we should not feel alone or less than. Even Bill W. experienced it after getting sober, and not for just a little while: "It was fortunate, for my old business associates remained skeptical for a year and a half, during which I found little work." But no one can say he did not make good use of this time: he threw himself into intensive work with other alcoholics, and his work resulted in the creation of Alcoholics Anonymous. He says about this time, and how his program buoyed him: "It is a design for living that works in rough going." He goes on to say something remarkable, maybe even hard to believe when we're in trouble of our own: "The joy of living we really have, even under pressure and difficulty."

Jobs can go; relationships can go; cars and houses and even loved ones. But in our program we have something no one can take away from us. No one can take our sobriety from us but us; no one can take our spiritual connection to a higher power away from us but us; and no one can take the program of Alcoholics Anonymous away from us but us. AA is something that we can have for keeps.

11 We will intuitively know how to handle situations which used to baffle us

There's an old AA joke that goes something like this: "It's a good thing I got into Alcoholics Anonymous, because my car was dying of alcoholism." I could have said that when I got in. My drinking robbed me of the ability to do things consistently, whether it was at work, at home, or changing the oil in my car. Only luck kept it from robbing me of much more. To me, it was an AA miracle the day my car was registered, inspected, and insured all at the same time. I found most of the mechanics of adult life baffling when I drank, whether it was filling out forms for school, taxes, or registering my car, and I had the disorganized, frustrating, running-from-crisis-to-crisis life that resulted from that.

It wasn't only my car that was dying of alcoholism. My marriage was dying of alcoholism; my relationship with my family and friends was dying of alcoholism; my career and even my ability to work was dying of alcoholism. But I didn't know that: I didn't know that because my disease was killing me last. Like a lot of alcoholics, I had a really hard time connecting the dots between my problems and my drinking. Sure, I knew that my drinking caused problems when I was drunk, but what about the times when I didn't have a glass in my hand? I went to doctors and psychiatrists, counselors for my relationships, lawyers for fixes I found myself in, and was confused about why I always seemed to have bosses that had it in for me. I looked at other people who seemed to be able to handle adult life and thought: "Why can they handle it and not me? What's wrong with me?"

Above all, I was baffled and frightened by the turn my drinking had taken. Waking up sick in the morning, I'd say to myself: "I really need to lay off for awhile." But then by 3 P.M., it was as if I'd never had that thought. Later on, when I got into AA and got to read our literature, I learned that this kind of mental blind spot concerning alcohol was common among alcoholics: "And the truth, strange to say, is usually that he has no more idea why he took that first drink than you have…Once this malady has a real hold, they are a baffled lot."

The end result of my drinking, our literature tells me, is

Thirteen Promises

really common too, as Bill says in an offhand way of his 12th step visit to a sick alcoholic: "It was the usual situation: home in jeopardy, wife ill, children distracted, bills in arrears and standing damaged." It was the usual situation, and by the time I found myself in it, I was truly baffled about how to get out. It was not as if I had tried countless ways to fix me and my life. But while therapy, medication, meditation, switching jobs, locations and relationships sometimes helped a little, I was soon back in the same miserable mess. Those solutions didn't work because none of them were a cure for alcoholism, and I was too baffled to realize that it was my drinking that was fueling most if not all of the other problems in my life. Ultimately I reached the same place described by Bill in the Big Book here: "We were in a position where life was becoming impossible, and if we had passed into the region from which there is no return through human aid, we had but two alternatives: One was to go on to the bitter end, blotting out the consciousness of our intolerable situation as best we could: and the other, to accept spiritual help."

Spiritual help? What's that?! I thought. Like many members of AA I did not have a strong religious faith or connection to a higher power when I arrived at the doorstep of my first meeting. I sometimes envied people who did have that kind of connection, and wished I had the kind of comfort and direction it seemed to give them. I still find it hard to summarize what I do believe today, and it would be fair to say that I have lots of beliefs but little certainty. But I try to remember that faith is not certainty. If I hold out the cup of coffee on my writing table and drop it, I am certain that it will drop to the floor, and not float up to the ceiling. But that's not faith: that's certainty. Faith requires a little more work, since ways to prove it are often beyond our reach.

After countless bad mornings where I swore off drinking, for a little while or forever, only to find myself drinking without my own permission days or even just hours later, I realized that I had to have help. It seemed silly to me -- why couldn't I just get over it on my own? I didn't realize what I was up against, but by going to AA, I met people who did. "Remember we deal with alcohol -- cunning, baffling, powerful!" our book says. "Without help it is too much for us."

Since I didn't know God all that well at the beginning, my first help came from other members of AA, who seemed to understand me, who would listen to my troubles with real sympathy and understanding, and who told me things in simple ways that really helped me. One that's stuck with me came from a member I heard speak in a meeting, where she said, "There are thousands of situations, but only one problem. I have only one problem: that's my alcoholism. Everything else is just a situation. And if I take good care of my alcoholism, those situations will pass. Situations come and situations go: that's what they do. So it would be pointless to drink over them. Worse than pointless, since drinking would only make matters even more difficult."

This was the kind of vital information I needed, directly from other people who had faced the same problems, once I got sober. Because it's not like I got sober and stopped having "situations." In fact, there are times when they seem to pile up on me in a way that seems really unreasonable and unfair.

Today when I have a problem I know that I'm not alone, and I have tools to help me approach the changes and difficulties of my life. One of the most powerful of these is the Serenity Prayer:

, grant me the serenity to accept the things I cannot change,
The courage to change the things I can,
And the wisdom to know the difference.

The Serenity Prayer is great in those tough moments, and I do use it that way, but I also use it as a decision making tool. The Serenity Prayer helps me figure out what kind of problem I have, which goes a long way towards reducing my bafflement about it. Do I have a Line One problem -- is there something in my life that I can't change and need to accept? Is it a Line Two problem -- something that I need to work on to change? Or is it impossible for me to tell whether it's something I should accept or try to change? In that case, it's a Line Three problem, and I need to pray for the wisdom to tell the difference.

For many years, I ran the Serenity Prayer in the reverse in my life. If I needed to accept it, I railed against it and tried to force my own will; if it was something I should change, well, that looked like work, and I wasn't all that interested in work, and if I didn't know what I should do, well, I just waded on in there anyway. I'd figure it out, right? Well, I had the life that resulted from that, which I'm sure you can imagine (or maybe remember!).

I often have problems today that put me in a situation where I'm not sure what the next right action is. Our program offers hints for this: "In thinking about our day we may face indecision. We may not be able to determine which course to take. Her we ask God for inspiration, an intuitive thought or a decision. We relax and take it easy. We don't struggle. We are often surprised how the right answers come after we have tried this for awhile. What used to be the hunch or the occasional inspiration gradually becomes a working part of the mind." You may find, as many of us have, that our intuition sharpens as we gain more sober time under our belt. While drinking or using, we were often guided by our paranoia, but since that was our disease and not reality talking, it rarely kept us out of trouble for long. Our god-given ability to get hunches and develop intuitions from real-world situations becomes much better when it isn't being dulled by alcohol. In sobriety, I've been able to avoid troublesome situations because I am cleared up enough to hear those quiet intuitions. Even the sense of awe and wonder, that goosebumps feeling, has come back to me in sobriety.

Thirteen Promises

Sometimes we know that we must change something, or must accept it, but we're just not sure how. This is where the practical experience of millions of sober alcoholics, the ones we meet in our own meeting halls or the ones who have left their most important advice behind, can help us. We need to hear from other alcoholics not just how but why to do the difficult work of changing or accepting; that's where the wisdom comes from.

"And acceptance is the answer to *all* my problems today. When I am disturbed, it is because I find some person, place, thing, or situation -- some fact of my life -- unacceptable to me, and I can find no serenity until I accept that person, place, thing, or situation as being exactly the way it is supposed to be at this moment. Until I could accept my alcoholism, I could not stay sober; unless I accept life completely on life's terms, I cannot be happy. I need to concentrate not so much on what needs to be changed in the world as on what needs to be changed in me and my attitudes."

I'm grateful today for the wisdom I have gotten from other sober men and women who have traveled the path before me, and I want to share my experience with others in hopes that it can help another alcoholic deal with the problems life may hand them today.

Thirteen Promises

12   We will suddenly realize that God is doing for us what we could not do for ourselves

When Bill W. recounts his story, he tells us about a time when he was still drinking, and an old friend -- someone who drank like he did -- came to visit. By this time, Bill had already been hospitalized twice for his alcoholism, but was drinking again. Things were bad: he needed to hide bottles near his bed to help with the shakes when he'd wake; he was out of work and his wife was trying to support them as a sales clerk at a department store. Perhaps because things were so bleak, Bill was really looking forward to his friend's visit, even though he'd heard that his friend had gotten sober. "His coming was an oasis in the dreary desert of futility. The very thing -- an oasis! Drinkers are like that."

Bill is amazed that his friend has been able to stop and stay stopped -- something he hasn't yet been able to do himself. How did he do it? "...My friend sat before me, and he made the point-blank declaration that God had done for

Thirteen Promises

him what he could not do for himself."

Only those of us who have picked up a drink when we swore we wouldn't, drank when we shouldn't, drank in ways that prevented us from parenting our kids, had a DUI and drank after, lost a job and drank after, lost a relationship...and still drank; those of us who have experienced the hopelessness and futility of drinking without our own permission -- only we can truly understand what it means to be trapped by our addiction, to be in too deep to get out on our own.

Sometimes people have tried to help us. Sometimes this "help" did not take the most pleasant form. Sometimes they screamed at us, or tried to get us to stop by threatening to take things away -- or actually taking things away. Sometimes they threatened to leave us, or put us out on the street, or call the police, and sometimes they did. Some tried to help in ways that seemed more gentle or more constructive, by trying to get us into treatment, or to give therapy another try. Yet we often treated the people who tried to help us to our most awful behavior, even sometimes blaming them for our drinking, shouting at them that if they'd only do this or that we'd stop. All this "help," especially from non-alcoholics, didn't usually help us stop drinking.

There's a simple reason why this help wasn't helpful: ordinary humans make lousy Gods, and alcoholism is a disease that is more than just mental and physical: it is a spiritual malady which requires a spiritual solution. Whether that is service, the community spirit within the rooms of AA, the quiet but powerful coincidences we experience in sobriety, or a deity of your own understanding, some sort of connection to something bigger than ourselves seems to be required for us to recover fully from drinking.

Yet even when we prayed for it, we could not stop drinking. That's because we never suddenly realize that God is doing for us what we *can* do for ourselves, and it is up to us to get to our first meeting and keep going.

Sure, alcoholism is both mental and physical, but if it were not something more, we'd have cured it long ago with medical or psychological therapies. What kind of disease made people who had it lie, cheat, and steal? Other

Thirteen Promises

diseases, like eczema or diabetes, did not find their sufferers waking up in the wrong bed with the wrong people, or waking up in dread only to read awful messages they'd sent. ==That's because unlike other illnesses, alcoholism has a spiritual dimension.==

Bill senses that more has happened to his friend than just putting down the drink. He's not just "not drinking" -- he's changed. "There was something about his eyes. He was inexplicably different." After hearing about his friend's experience in sobriety, he says, "I saw that my friend was much more than inwardly changed. His roots grasped a new soil."

Here's the secret that many alcoholics come to know: sobriety is much more than just not drinking. ==It is the kind of spiritual growth that lets us do new things, starting with staying sober but extending in all directions out into our lives.== For those of us who remember those awful times when we were drunk and said exactly the wrong thing, something incredibly mean or cruel, before we even realized we'd said it, we now find ourselves saying good things we had no idea we were about to say: words of forgiveness, words of kindness and courtesy even to people

Thirteen Promises

who have wronged us.

We have already experienced the miracle of not having to drink, and as we work the steps we experience the miracle of being able to act in a way where we can be proud of ourselves and like ourselves -- all things we hadn't been able to manage before, no matter how hard we tried. I sometimes feel so different from the "me" I was when I was drinking that I wonder if Old Me died and I just got all her stuff.

There are times God does for me things I cannot do for myself and I'm not happy about it. I rarely let go of anything unless it has claw marks on it. I am the poster child for "Let Go, Or Be Dragged." But God has been very insistent on plucking me out of relationships that were not going to work, or jobs that weren't going to work out, or making sure the place I wanted to live was already rented because he had something else for me in mind.

Some of these losses were intensely painful, but at some point, often quite quickly, I see that God had simply removed me from a train that was about to go off the rails in a spectacular crash. It would be pretty churlish of me to be saved from disaster and complain that I had to get off before my stop.

"When we look back we realize that the things which came to us when we put ourselves in God's hands were better than anything we could have planned," it says in the Big Book. I have found this to be true in my own life, and hope that you find it to be true in yours.

Are these extravagant promises?

Hell yes!

13   They are being fulfilled among us, sometimes quickly, sometimes slowly. They will always materialize if we work for them

A woman I know in the program often says, "We stay sober and we do the work and the gifts come. No one gets skipped."

But what does it mean to work for those gifts? It means that staying sober is not enough. It is necessary, it is critical, but it is not enough. We must do the work of recovery, first by working the Twelve Steps. We cannot expect to be granted the 9th step promises when we're unwilling to sit down and finish our fourth step inventory, or if we're dawdling on setting a time to sit down with a sponsor and do a 5th step.

A sober life is a beautiful life, but it can also sometimes be a challenging life. If the prospect of the steps frighten you, remember what the Big Book tells us happens after we complete step 5 — we get a new boss: "We had a new Employer. Being all powerful, He provided what we needed, if we kept close to him and performed his work well." In times of trouble and uncertainty, this can be a real comfort. We're not working for the boss, or to impress anyone; everything we could ever need to succeed at the work of recovery is always within our grasp — God put it there and keeps it there.

If we are willing to work at our recovery, the "simple kit of spiritual tools" is always at the ready. When things are bad, we can remember that our primary purpose isn't to pay bills or get our kid into the right school or get ourselves into the right relationship: our primary purpose is to stay sober and help another alcoholic. We can do this work under any and all circumstances; we can do it when we have a job or when we're unemployed; we can do it in times of peace or times of war; we can do it in good times and in lean ones; we can do it when we have one day sober or 42 years sober.

When I first got sober, people repeated the basics to me often: "Don't drink, go to meetings, and ask for help." When I'd been doing that for awhile, I began to hear, "and when you're ready for your life to get better, join a group, get a sponsor, and work the steps."

Doing so means more than just getting ourselves on the path to the Promises coming true in our lives. Having an active program of recovery — attending meetings regularly, having a home group, having a sponsor, working the steps, and doing service work in the program — is an insurance policy. We can't kid ourselves about the dangers of cutting corners in our recovery. Putting off that fourth or fifth step for later, letting meetings slide, or letting your relationship with your sponsor be less important to you than watching something on Netflix are a recipe for relapse. Even in 1939, our fellow alcoholics knew this: "For if an alcoholic failed to perfect and enlarge his spiritual life through work and self-sacrifice for others, he could not survive the certain trials and low spots ahead. If he did not work, he would surely drink again, and if he drank, he would surely die. Then faith would be dead indeed. With us it is just like that."

With us, it is just like that.

We could feel bad that this is the way it is. We could feel bad that we have to do the work. Or we could tune in to the "normal" people in our lives and notice that many of them aren't doing that well. Alcoholics are a funny people:

==unlike normal folk, we actually cannot stay stuck, stay miserable, stay blaming others and avoiding responsibility== — if we do, we drink, and if we drink, we die.

We are lucky because we don't have the option to remain in denial — not just about alcohol but about anything in our lives. We can't remain in denial about the relationship, the job, the living situation, our habits, attitudes, or our character, because remaining in denial about any of those things may bring us back to the point where nothing but Higher-Power fueled coincidence will keep us from drinking or using.

We are also lucky, unbelievably lucky, because we belong to a movement that gives us a design for living that really works, even in rough going. I would bet that all of us have been involved in things — jobs, organizations, relationships — that did not give us as much back as we put into it. But AA is not a racket: whatever we put into our recovery will come back to us, with interest. Let us invest in ourselves, each other, our world, our recovery. May the work we do in our hearts, in the rooms, in our inventory, in our amends, ripple out to touch our loved ones, our communities, and our world. There is nothing, absolutely nothing that this world needs more than an army of sober women who are alive, awake, and present, women of honor, dignity and integrity who will do what they say they are going to do, who show up when and where they say they will, who have the confidence that comes from knowing they can do hard things because they have already done the first and best hard thing: getting and staying sober.

A Brief Guide to AA Jargon

Alcathon -- an event, typically on a holiday such as Thanksgiving, Christmas, or New Year's Eve/Day, or 4th of July, where a regional AA group works to put on an event with back-to-back meetings lasting all day and sometimes through an entire 24 hour period. Intended to help people get through difficult holidays but also provide people a break from holiday and family stresses with easy-to-access meetings.

Al-Anon -- A 12-step program for the families of alcoholics.

Amends -- The 9th step reads: "Made direct amends to such people wherever possible, except when to do so would injure them or others." An amends is a sincere effort to make right the harm we have done others. It is more than an apology: an amends "mends" things.

Anniversary -- The yearly anniversary of your sobriety date. In some places, this is called a birthday.

AWOL — If you're hearing this in a meeting, and a veteran of military service is not telling their story from the podium, it doesn't mean "Absent Without Leave." It means "A Way of Life," and it's a structured way of taking a group of people through the 12 Steps.

Big Book -- The book "Alcoholics Anonymous," from which the fellowship takes its name, is typically referred to as "The Big Book."

Big Book Step Study -- A structured way of moving through the steps. Groups following this pattern are popular in the Northeast US.

Central Service — The offices of a local Intergroup of Alcoholics Anonymous. Central Service typically runs a phone hotline and makes meeting lists available. To find an AA meeting in your area, type "my city name AA" into Google and you will likely be able to find the phone number of your local Central Service office, who can help you locate a meeting near you.

Chip -- a small metal or plastic token denoting a length of sobriety from 24 hours to 11 months.

Coin -- Another word for a chip or medallion.

Clubhouse — In some regions of the US, it's common to have clubhouses where 12 step meetings are held throughout the day. Many also provide a safe, sober space to hang out in between meetings. Sometimes called Alano Clubs, but go by many different names.

Commitment -- An exchange where members of one group travel to another group to speak at that meeting. Some groups have commitments to bring AA meetings into hospitals and institutions.

Convention -- A large, multiday AA gathering with workshops and talks. Many districts have their own annual conventions. AA's International Convention happens every five years.

Counting days -- When someone says they are "counting days," they are in the early part of sobriety where they are still keeping track of each additional day of sobriety. Many people "count days" for the first 90, 100, or 365 days.

Thirteen Promises

Crosstalk -- many meetings ask members to avoid crosstalk. But what is it? Crosstalk is when you address another member by name during a meeting, giving them advice or your feelings about what they said. In general, you should speak from *your own experience* about *what's happening with you* in an AA meeting. Some meetings are more relaxed about crosstalk, while other meetings actually have formats that encourage it. But in general, at a new meeting you should assume that crosstalk is discouraged.

Dry drunk -- someone who is not drinking, but does not have a program of recovery involving the 12 steps or any other recovery tradition. When people speak of being a 'dry drunk' they are often referring to the anger, mood swings, and impulsiveness that affects many alcoholics who stop drinking but do nothing else to recover.

Detox — A medical ward in a hospital where people are withdrawn safely from alcohol and other drugs.

Get-well job -- Some people may choose to get a less-challenging job -- one that pays the bills but isn't too stressful and allows plenty of time for meetings -- during their first year in sobriety in order to focus on recovery.

Halfway house — a structured living environment for people exiting detox treatment at a hospital or rehab. Typically 6 months to a year, these group living environments encourage daily recovery activities, getting a job, and staying sober.

Home group — Recovering people are encouraged to pick a home group that they attend without fail. An old AA joke goes like this: "You only miss your home group if you are going to a funeral — your funeral." Recovery is aided by having people see you and people you see regularly. They get to know you, your struggles, and your progress. It's good to get a "job" (coffeemaker, secretary, etc) at your group and attend your group's business meeting (typically a short monthly meeting to handle things like paying the rent on the meeting space and ordering new books, etc).

Identifying as an alcoholic -- Saying "My name is (your name) and I'm an alcoholic" in a meeting of Alcoholics Anonymous.

Intergroup -- a regional AA organization. Typically an

intergroup prints meeting books and makes sure literature is available for groups. Many intergroups also run a hotline, sometimes 24 hours, where people can call with questions or ask for help finding a meeting. Intergroups do not make referrals to treatment centers.

Inventory -- Refers to the 4th Step inventory. An inventory is typically a written inventory which is then shared with one's sponsor as part of a person's 5th step. For a sense of what an inventory looks like and what it contains, see page 65 of the Big Book.

Medallion -- a metal token, typically larger and more solid than a chip, denoting a year or number of years of sobriety. Many have the AA symbol and a number showing the number of years on the front, and the Serenity Prayer on the back.

Old-Timer -- Someone with many years of sobriety.

PAWS — Post Acute Withdrawal Syndrome. Some people continue to experience symptoms after the initial few days or weeks of withdrawal from alcohol that include mood swings, difficulty sleeping, difficulty concentrating, cravings, and changes in appetite or energy level.

Pigeon -- Another word for "sponsee."

Qualify -- A person "qualifies" when they volunteer to lead off a meeting by telling their story, typically for 15-20 minutes.

Resentment -- the memory of a time when someone treated you in a way that made you feel bad.

Roundup -- Another word for a convention. Roundups are often, but not always, conventions by and for LGBT members of AA.

Sobriety date -- The date of your first sober day.

Sponsor -- A sponsor's primary responsibility is to take his or her sponsees through the 12 Steps. In addition, a sponsor often provides advice and guidance.

Step meeting -- A meeting which focuses on one or more of the 12 steps. Typically, a chapter of "Twelve Steps and Twelve Traditions" is read, and then members discuss their experience with that step or what they got from the reading. A good introduction to the Steps.

Turnarounds — the part of one's written 4th step inventory where we try to see our part in our resentments — what did we do to contribute to a painful situation with another person?

90 in 90 -- Many people recommend that newcomers to AA attend ninety meetings in ninety days. I'm one of those people. It's a good idea.

11th **step meeting** -- a meeting where meditation, rather than sharing, speaking or literature is the main event.

12&12 -- Refers to the book "Twelve Steps and Twelve Traditions," a series of essays about each of the steps and the traditions.

The 12 Traditions -- The 12 Steps are actions that individual members of AA take; the 12 Traditions guide how groups function.

12th Step Call — two sober people paying a visit to an alcoholic who has not gotten sober yet to tell their story of how they recovered.

How to pick your first AA meeting

Maybe you are reading this book, and you're pretty sure you have a drinking problem. Maybe you're still drinking. Maybe you've stopped, but you're having a hard time staying stopped. And maybe all this is happening with you, but you haven't gone to an AA meeting because — well for a lot of reasons, but let's just pick one that's true for a lot of us: you haven't gone yet because it's scary.

That's normal, by the way. It's normal to be scared. Sobriety turns out to be a lot more than just putting down the drink: for me, and for many of us, it changes our lives in a way we can't predict or control, in ways that are much bigger and more far-reaching than simply leaving behind alcohol and the trouble it caused us. It is a big deal, going to your first AA meeting.

But if you think you are ready, I am going to tell you how to pick your first AA meeting. First, I'll tell you about my first AA meeting.

On the day of my first AA meeting, I needed to get a job

and a place to live real quick. If I didn't, I would lose access to my two kids.

Despite that fact, I stood out on the sidewalk in front of my first AA meeting thinking, "Am I overreacting?" It's funny. If strawberries did a fraction of the damage to our lives and communities that alcohol did, there would be people marching in the streets demanding that we burn all the fields. It's also funny how many of us have people around us who seem perfectly okay with us drinking ourselves to death (as long as our behavior doesn't inconvenience them) but go to a meeting, and you get the "Go to a MEETING?! You must have a REAL PROBLEM!" reaction. We live in a world that has a backwards and upside-down view of alcohol, and we can't help but carry some or a lot of those attitudes with us into our first meeting.

Fortunately, while standing out there on the sidewalk I had the first of what I think of as spiritual experiences: I suddenly had a thought in my head that felt like it wasn't me thinking it. It felt that way because this thought felt cool and composed and organized — and I was a hot mess.

That thought said: "Elle, do you think there's an

alcoholic Olympics? Do you want to go for the gold? Do you want to overachieve your way into Alcoholics Anonymous? Do you think you'll go up there and they'll give you an aptitude test and you'll flunk? Do you think they'll say, "Okay kid, go out and screw up your life for another couple of years, and then maybe you can get in"?

It doesn't work that way. Thank God it doesn't work that way. I didn't know this at the time, because I didn't know much about AA, but the only requirement for membership is a desire to stop drinking, and as I went in there, scared and sad and frightened, I had it.

So here's the thing: I picked a terrible first AA meeting.

It was tiny — in a conference room in an office building. It lacked one thing that is absolutely vital for a first AA meeting: a back row to hide in.

I cried through the entire meeting. I did not have tissues or a handkerchief — I was not remotely together enough to carry around things like that on my first day sober.

I don't remember much of what was said at that

meeting, but I do remember that when the meeting was over and we went out in the hallway, someone clapped me on the back and said, "Good honest tears in there."

God bless AA: it's the only place you can cry for an hour and people will praise you for keeping it real. Then a woman in the meeting said the most important thing to me: "We're going to be here again tomorrow. Come back."

I shrugged and mumbled something noncommittal, tears still falling as I couldn't seem to stop them.

"No," she said. "Say you'll come back."

And I did. And I went. I have been sober ever since. So maybe it wasn't such a bad first AA meeting. But I'm going to try to give you a sense of how to pick a first meeting that will minimize — but not eliminate, because we really can't — the scary and challenging parts of your first AA meeting.

First, type the name of your town or the nearest city and "AA Meetings" into Google.

You'll be able to find the website of your local AA

organization, and on that website they will have a meeting list.

Now, not all AA meetings are the same. They have different formats, are aimed at different groups of people, and go on for different lengths of time.

Some meeting lists will have acronyms, like "O," "SD," "12S." "SDGW" and more. Other meeting lists will spell those out, which is a little easier, but still doesn't tell you what those terms mean about the meetings you see listed.

O generally stands for "Open." An open meeting of Alcoholics Anonymous is one that's open to the public. Anyone can go to one, including friends and family members who don't have a drinking problem. Sometimes medical or nursing students attend one as part of their education. Even though non-alcoholics are invited to attend these meetings, they are asked not to speak or participate — just listen.

C generally stands for "Closed." That's a meeting where we ask that only people who feel they have a problem with drinking attend and participate.

M, W, LGBT — there are meetings for men, women, and LGBT people. I can't emphasize enough how important womens' meetings have been to my recovery. I urge you to get to one if you can. But it's more important to get to *a* meeting than it is to get to the "right" meeting.

For your first meeting, it might be best to choose an open speaker meeting. Most of the time, these meetings consist of a series of speakers getting up and telling their story. Many are not what is called a "participation meeting" — so you don't have to raise your hand to talk, and in most cases, people don't go around the room and say, "My name is X and I'm an alcoholic." At these meetings, all you have to do is sit and listen.

You do not have to be sober to attend your first meeting. Yes, you heard me right. The only requirement for membership in AA is a *desire* to stop drinking. In fact, every once in awhile will see people who are intoxicated at a meeting. They are welcome in the rooms of Alcoholics Anonymous. We are not here only for people who already fixed their problem: we're here for everyone who has a problem with drinking, including people who haven't stopped or are struggling to stay stopped. Everyone is to be treated with courtesy and kindness. In general, people are only asked to leave if they are disrupting a meeting.

You can bring your children to some meetings of Alcoholics Anonymous. Womens' meetings in particular are often sympathetic and friendly to mothers who want to get into recovery. Bring some headphones and something else to keep your kid busy. Every meeting is a little different, and some have rules about this. This is a case where it may be worth calling the phone number on the same site you found the meeting list on. Most regional AA organizations have a telephone line you can call. Use it! The person on the other end of the line is someone who has had the same troubles that you do. Tell them you want to get to a meeting and let them help you problem-solve your way to one that you can get to.

What to do in your first meeting

Identify, don't compare. You may hear this in meetings, but what does it mean? It means to listen with your heart. It means listening to the feelings that the speaker had about their drinking and about their recovery, rather than getting distracted by the particular circumstances of their bottom. It's very easy to talk your way right out of recovery by going to a meeting, listening to the story of someone who had a rougher bottom than you, and say "I'm not that bad — they're a real alcoholic. I'm fine, I just need more therapy, babysitting, yoga, stress relief, a different job, relationship, or for my husband to help more." Or you might be in a meeting and think, "I can't relate to these people -- nothing happened to them!" Remember that a bottom is a spiritual and emotional bottom. That can happen in a swanky suburban home or in a jail cell. It's not the surroundings that matter — it's the feelings — the terror, bewilderment, frustration and despair that finally bring us to the jumping-off point.

Don't expect everybody to be a great public speaker. While people underestimate the entertainment value of AA meetings, and some speakers are great storytellers who are very funny and moving, most are regular people who are standing in front of you telling you about one of the hardest things in their whole life. Listen with a generous heart.

Don't worry about paying for anything. Nobody cares if you put a dollar in the basket that is passed at meetings or not. Coffee and cookies at meetings are almost always free, too.

Don't expect online meetings to do the trick. The internet will not get you sober. Neither will Facebook.

Say you're new. Tell people this is your first meeting. Let them know you're new.

It works when you participate. Sobriety is not a spectator sport. As hard as it is, you have to raise your hand and let us know what's going on with you so we can get to know you and begin to understand how we can help you establish a program of recovery.

Get a meeting book or some literature if you can. Some meetings will have a pocket-sized listing of local meetings. The internet is great, but sometimes having something you can stick in a pocket and flip through is better. Sometimes members of a group will circle meetings they recommend in your area or write their phone numbers in a meeting book for you. Many groups will give you a copy of the "Big Book." If they do, take it. Our program's literature is perhaps not the most exciting in the world, but it's great for those early-sobriety times when you wake up at three in the morning freaked out about something.

Sit with the women. If you're scared, or some of the people in your meeting look a little rough, sit with the women.

How To Start A Promises Meeting

I was introduced to The Promises by attending a women's AA meeting where we discussed one of the Promises each week. There's just no way to understate the amount of insight and connection I have gotten from meditating on what each of these promises mean to me, and hearing how they have come true (or not) in other women's lives.

You can use any format that is customary to your group. In ours, we begin with a moment of silence, the AA preamble, and then we pass around a sheet with each of the Promises numbered. A woman reads one of the 13 promises, and passes it on to the next person until all the Promises are read.

At that point, the chair reads out that week's Promise. The discussion begins when one woman raises her hand, and after her share on that week's Promise, she gets to pick a direction — should the person to her left or right speak first? The discussion continues around the circle until everyone has had a chance to speak or time is up.

Here's a sample format you can adapt for your own use. For a printable version, visit bit.ly/promises-meeting where you can download a PDF to print out.

Thirteen Promises

Promises Meeting Format

Hello and welcome to [your group name]. We begin this meeting with a moment of silence.

This is the AA preamble: Alcoholics Anonymous is a fellowship of men and women who share their experience, strength and hope with each other that they may solve their common problem and help others to recover from alcoholism. The only requirement for membership is a desire to stop drinking. There are no dues or fees for A.A. membership; we are self-supporting through our own contributions. A.A. is not allied with any sect, denomination, politics, organization or institution; does not wish to engage in any controversy, neither endorses nor opposes any causes. Our primary purpose is to stay sober and help other alcoholics to achieve sobriety.

This meeting is a discussion of The Promises, which appear on pages 83 and 84 of the Big Book of Alcoholics Anonymous. Please read one promise and then pass to your right.

[Pass the printout of the Promises to your right].

Discussion will begin by a show of hands and proceed around the circle.

[After the first person has shared, ask her to pick a direction for sharing to continue].

Listen

One of the most remarkable things about our movement is that it happened entirely during the era of recording. If you want to hear the voices and stories and laughter of our founders, you can. Since those early recordings, alcoholics doing acts of service have amassed a treasure trove of tens of thousands of hours of recordings of alcoholics telling you their stories: what happened, what it was like, and what it's like now.

Remember that there are no substitutes for an in-person meeting of Alcoholics Anonymous — Facebook groups, the internet, or recorded meetings are all great as extras, but they are not a basis for a solid program of recovery. But talks like the ones below and many more can be a great complement to your program, to long drives, and to tough days.

Women speakers

Lila R. (http://www.recoveryaudio.org/speaker/lila-r)
Megan M. (http://xa-speakers.org/pafiledb.php?

action=file&id=456)

Lorna K. (www.recoveryaudio.org/aa-speaker-tapes/atlantic-group-lorna-k-2006)

Polly P. (xa-speakers.org/pafiledb.php?action=file&id=363)

Patti O. (xa-speakers.org/pafiledb.php?action=file&id=1214)

Angie P. (www.recoveryaudio.org/aa-speaker-tapes/angie-p-cincinnati-oh-46th-womens-conf-fl-2010)

Joe and Charlie

Joe and Charlie were two recovered alcoholics from the South, one black and one white, who toured the US doing their "Big Book Comes Alive" show, taking us through the Big Book in a friendly and entertaining way. They're so endearing that it's hard not to want them as part of your sober family once you've listened to these.

Joe and Charlie's Big Book Comes Alive series (www.xa-speakers.org/pafiledb.php?action=file&id=150)

AA's cofounders: Bill W. & Dr. Bob

Bill. W: Here's Bill speaking at the Texas State AA convention in 1954. He has a distinctive voice and style of speaking. (www.xa-speakers.org/pafiledb.php?action=file&id=1371)

Dr. Bob: Here he is speaking in Detroit in 1948, recounting the story of his meeting with Bill W. (www.recoveryaudio.org/aa-speaker-tapes/dr-bob-smith-history-and-recovery-story-detroit-mi-1948)

Hear the voices of early members of Alcoholics Anonymous and authors of stories in the Big Book:

Lyle P., pilot and author of the Big Book story "Grounded." (mirror.xa-speakers.org/speakers/aa/single-speakers/lyle-p/lyle-p-bbstory-grounded128.mp3)

Dr. Paul O., author of "Acceptance Was The Answer," which contains the famous passage on acceptance. (www.recoveryaudio.org/speaker/dr-paul-o)

Marty M., author of the Big Book story "Women Suffer Too." (www.recoveryaudio.org/aa-speaker-tapes/bb-author-of-women-suffer-too-marty-mann-dos-1939-recorded-1966)

Beth H., author of the Big Book story "Empty on the Inside." (www.recoveryaudio.org/aa-speaker-tapes/

footprints-in-the-winter-sand-ocean-city-md-2005)

Earl M., author of "Physician, Heal Thyself." (www.recoveryaudio.org/aa-speaker-tapes/dr-earl-m-the-author-of-big-book-story-phsician-heal-thyself)

Wynn L., author of "Freedom From Bondage." (xa-speakers.org/pafiledb.php?action=file&id=1492)

Classic AA Speakers

Clancy I. — A longtime circuit speaker who was a successful advertising writer but ended up getting sober while living in an abandoned car. Once getting sober, he ran an outreach service in Los Angeles. A funny and incisive speaker who talks a lot about rebuilding our lives in sobriety. (wejoy.org/php/speaker_detail.php?slug=clancy_i_atlanta_1982&keyword=clancy)

Chuck C. — Talks about rebuilding his family in sobriety. His "A New Set Of Glasses" talks cover being sober and making a living. (wejoy.org/php/speaker_detail.php?slug=chuck-c-5&keyword=chuck+c)

Sandy B. — From drinking in his surf shop to sobering

up as a teacher, Sandy B is both funny and touching. (wejoy.org/php/speaker_detail.php?slug=sandy_b_jekyll_1999&keyword=sandy+b)

Barry L., an early LGBT member of AA, good friend of Bill W.'S wife Lois, and author of Living Sober. (www.recoveryaudio.org/aa-speaker-tapes/barry-l-from-new-york-ny-speaking-at-the-50th-world-conference-in-montreal-in-july-1985-barry-is-the-author-of)

Scott R., a television writer and comic, gives a wonderful look at the 4th step. (www.recoveryaudio.org/speaker/scott-r)

Don G., a judge, is just too funny to pass up. (www.recoveryaudio.org/speaker/judge-don-g)

Where to find more recordings of people telling their recovery stories:

XA-Speakers: http://xa-speakers.org
RecoveryAudio: http://recoveryaudio.com
WeJoy: http://wejoy.org

About this book

Denise Chapeton of New Orleans, Louisiana, designed the cover of this book. You can reach her at: deecee1205@gmail.com.

Elle is just another woman in recovery living in Massachusetts.

Made in the USA
Middletown, DE
14 February 2024

49736014R00066